How to get involved in Orisha

with no added stress

Baba Sixto J. Novaton

blue ocean press

tokyo - florida

Published by: blue ocean press, an imprint of Aoishima Research Institute

U.S. (Main) Office

P.O. Box 510818

Punta Gorda, Florida 33951

807-36 Lions Plaza Ebisu

3-25-3 Higashi, Shibuya-ku, Tokyo, Japan 150

Email: contact@blueoceanpublications.com

URL: http://www.blueoceanpublications.com

ISBN: 978-4-902837-99-5

Table of Contents

Introduction

Before an individual becomes a godchild, they should be attended to for the sole purpose of getting their life in order. This does not imply giving them entities or initiations right away, especially without them knowing what they are getting into. Individuals need a series of strong ritual work to get rid of the negative karma that they have been exposed to since birth. This is accomplished through consistent readings and ritual work for a period-of-time, along with support in understanding how spirituality works and connecting to it effectively. Hence, this is not an overnight or simple process.

Step 01

Individuals should be attended by (Olorisha or Babalawo) priest in the first year at least three or more times, or once every three months; in essence - with every change of season.

The first few readings are to identify the negative karma and the traumas they have experienced. These investigations are necessary so that proper and correct work (spiritual healing therapy solutions) is performed in expunging all the negatives on route towards securing positive occurrences. People do not realize that ritual is necessary for every traumatic event in their life. The energies or influenza of experienced tragedies stay imbedded in their aura, psyche, and consciousness, and it takes quite a few healings to release bad karma associated with these events (causes & effects). Also, to be expunged is negative DNA passed down from birth, as well as, absorbed through bodily fluid transfers during sexual relations/experiences from current, previous failed, or casual relationships. People carry the energies of their previous lovers from one person to the next. Then, they wonder why - new relationships fail or don't last? Apparently, soap and water does not cleanse the powerful energy transfer that occurs within relationships...

Step 02

Olorisha priest/-ess or Babalawo should support the individual in the setting up of their spiritual shrine - so that they can begin to devote time to their enlightenment and connection to their spirit guides, ancestors, and other forces. This devotional process should take about 6 months to a year.

Step 03

Elders should then support the individual in having at least 2 spiritual masses that year (get good mediums), so that they can become aware of some of those spirit guides and ancestors closest to them. These have been listening to their prayers, and it is good to know that they have been receiving light (acknowledgement) or the power of the holy spirit. These spirits are of great asset and one day through subsequent readings will ask to be fed a libation or live animal per elder divination.

Step 04

The new godchild should next be taken to have their guardian Orisha marked - preferably by way of IFa (Ikin casting) - this should be done before even giving them elekes. Most elders rush and give elekes to people via default Orisha Obatala. But, they know that a more solid way is to place the eleke of the guardian Orisha last during ritual – when it is known.

Step 05

Now, that the individuals Orisha Guardian is known, Olorisha priests/-esses will know if they can continually attend the individual or not; depending upon the taboos or restrictions associated with the godparents' Orisha. Consequently, a responsible Olorisha priest/-ess will not continue with a godchild, if they are forbidden from touching the person's head. They, however can continue attending them as a spiritual advisor and spiritual godparent of sorts – but not take to the priesthood.

Step 06

It is very important that the individual bring a white plate with two coconuts, two candles and a small monetary offering to the Olorisha priest/-ess shrine. The Olorisha priest/-ess will break coconut(Obi) and toss to verify that their Orisha accepts the new godchild in the house.

Step 07

Next, they should have a Babalawo feed the egun of the Orisha that walks with the individual. Many people associate this divinity with Palo Mayombe, or spirit guide, or who's to say what other entity. But, it is not: it is the pure spiritual reflection of the guardian Orisha as an egun that walks with the individual - and facilitates the communication between the Orisha guardian and the individual (at their Ori (head) and Oyiyi (shadow) level). Its terminology is Egun Shebo (the egun of the orisha that walks with the individual (no name just title). If male Orisha it requires a male animal (fowl), if female Orisha female animal (fowl), i.e. male energy/female energy sacrifice.

Step 08

Now, that the godchild has their elekes, and they have fed the egun of the orisha that walks with them. They are to feed their guardian Orisha by way of their godparents' Orisha shrine, so that their godparents' Orisha recognizes the godchild's good heart and intentions. Example, If - you are a child of Oshun, you are to offer 2 hens to your godmother's Oshun from your heart out of respect to the Oshun of your godmother; because one day hopefully you will be initiated from this Orisha shrine.

Step 09

On another day from their heart, the godchild should offer two fowls to the guardian Orisha of their godparent out of love and respect to their godparent and the Orisha shrine. This way their guardian Orisha and the Orisha of their godparent are in tune with helping the new godchild get their life in order. And, support their forward progress towards Orisha priesthood.

By this stage 09 - if the Babalawo and priest have good Ashe - the person should have most of all their situations resolved. Hence, good job, roof over their head, a good mate or happy home - In essence, living well and on their way towards better things.

Step 10

Now, comes taking the individual to a Babalawo to receive their warriors (Eshu, Ogun/Oshosi/Ozun) or have them consecrated. These should be first - then the Olorisha priest should consecrate an Eleggua (solid stone no face) – Eshu satisfies arbitrary forces, crosses over to the dark-side, and egungun, while Eleggua satisfies arbitrary forces – but, doesn't cross over to the dark-side as Eshu does.

Step 11

Now that one has their warriors, the godparent can give them Yemaya-Olokun, Ibejis, and Orisha-Oko as needed (if feasible), and any other Orisha prior to Ocha – as the Olorisha priest/-ess readings determine or IFA readings dictates. These are auxiliary Orisha that support positive destinies in the godchild's life securing the economic well-being for them to eventually reach crowning Ocha. Also, if this is as far as the godchild is to come or willing to go – then so be it. Not everyone that enters Orisha worship has come to become initiated as priests/-esses.

Step 12

Now, take the godchild to receive the hand of IFa - this is the oracle of destiny. Orunmila marks an individual's destiny or walks of life – independent of having Ocha or not. This is important because the person will know before having Osha what they are up against in their life. Even if an individual makes Ocha their destiny does not change. Ocha enhances their well-being and gives them a purpose as priests/-esses in society as part of a fulfillment within their destiny. The Ocha Ita defines how each Ocha Orisha will support the destiny – but, the destiny is identified by way of Orunmila – casting IFa (Ikin divination).

Imagine how many people have Ocha, and do not have hand of IFa - this means that their destiny has not been made know to them – even when having Ocha.

I suggest that during the consecration of their hand of IFa - and since, IFa is speaking at that moment, and if they have not already been scratched in Palo. They should ask the question - if they need to be scratched in Palo by their hand through Ikin at that moment of receiving the oracle of destiny. Also, the Palo entity would automatically be the synchronized Orisha guardian. For Example - if a person is a child of Obatala - automatically they are Tiembla Tierra. If they are a child of Ogun – Sarabanda; Yemaya - Madre Agua - etc. Anything else other than the logical Orisha to be synchronized would mean confusion during the spiritual evolutionary process of the godchild.

I have seen to many cases of people scratched under the wrong Palo divinity - for example, a child of Obatala as Sarabanda, or a child of Elegua as Siete Rayo. This means that their Guardian Angel was not determined by IFa before taking them to Palo - and the proper investigations of affirmations did not take place. Hence, people being crossed between Egun and Orisha. This should not happen - If you are a child of Shango - automatically you are 7 Rayo; you shouldn't be anything else. People rush, don't take the necessary time, don't do adequate investigation, and unfortunately don't confer with IFa. Orunmila is always the last word, and will verify what you know or think you know.

Insight:

Many people receive warriors, hand of IFa, and marked Orisha guardian all at once. But, it does not necessarily have to be this way. For my godchildren, I have broken things up this way into 3 interval periods in time; 1st- Orisha guardian, 2nd warriors after elekes, and 3rd hand of Ifa later-on. This is so that the godchild does not incur a high cost all at once. Normally, its accomplished between a two to three- year period, or sooner depending on situation. Splitting things up and taking one's time is not as stringent on the godchild's pocket as otherwise. Also, gives time for the godchild to see results as they resolve the various complex situations of their life - in an interval period of while working, learning, developing spirituality, and living.

Orisha Practice is a life-long endeavor, if there isn't an emergency then take your time. Do as many cleanings (ebbos) as necessary you will experience many positive results – because you need proof. Proof is not obtained with one cleaning or receiving one thing only.

Step 13

Finally, Maintaining - this involves routinely once or twice a year feeding egungun, warriors, hand of Ifa (Orunmila) and other related Orisha - along with getting at least 2 readings and ebbos per year by godparents until they are ready to become priests/-esses.

Closing

Unfortunately, people come to Orisha in crisis mode (when there are problems), and then get used to working Orisha in crisis mode alone. But, it doesn't have to be this way. Once a person resolves their crisis situations, they should follow up with the Orisha priest Santero or Babalawo to always secure a blessed future. The hard part is not just in getting to where you are going or obtaining the things you need; it is maintaining what has taken so much hard work to obtain.

About Baba Sixto

Baba Sixto was born in Cuba in 1961, and brought to the United States in 1966, where has lived all his life. He was initiated into the Cuban Yoruba Lucumi Santeria Religion as a Shango priest in 1977. He worked as an IT professional from 1979 to 2000. Baba Sixto was initiated as a Yoruba Lucumi Ifa priest in 1997.

Dedicated to full-time religious study and practice, as an Ifa priest since 2000, Baba Sixto has instructed many on how to build spirituality, connect to spiritual forces, so as to acquire the necessary intonation to then enter the Yoruba Lucumi Religion. Working as a Babalawo, Baba Sixto supports the well-being of humankind through Yoruba Lucumi Ifa ritual healing therapies.

He currently lives and works in Jacksonville, Florida. He also travels and attends to his godchildren and clients in New York, Georgia, Texas, and Puerto Rico.

Botanica Monte Santo
1316 Cesery Blvd., Jacksonville, FL 32211
(904) 507-9440

Other Titles by Baba Sixto:

Yoruba 16 Oracle Geomancy
by Sixto J. Novaton
ISBN: 978-4-902837-16-2

Obtaining an oracle for divination from the coconut/ cowrie/ coin toss:

This simple system, developed with insights from the cowrie (dilogun) and Ifa systems of divination, is a written for those who after having dedicated much time to spiritual enlightenment, now have a need to verify their communication through a simple 'yes' or 'no' questioning system, plus a more elaborate simple binary extension. Plainly, there are those who do not have an affinity with any divination system.

Baba Sixto put together this system of 16 basic signs that will support the communication necessary for any individual to obtain answers. The rest is up to the individual's merited grace and intuition. This system will also expand an individual's medium development through devotion and practice. To be utilized are four circular coconut shells, 4 coins, or 4 cowrie shells. The objects need to be of the same type, shape, and one side can be identified as facing upward (1), and the bottom side (0).

In this book, Baba Sixto also provides readers with instructions on simple, but effective spiritual remedies such as: 1) setting up a spiritual altar, 2) generating a spiritual bath, 3) knowing how to influence people using spirituality, 4) knowing how to perform an exorcism using ashes, 5) how to overcome an evil spirit, 6) simple ground feeding ritual, 7) simple door feeding, 8) spiritual baths to expunge negative influence and attract positive energies, 9) simple love spell, 10) protection against enemies, 11) simple head washing ritual.

Selected Prayers for Enlightenment
by Sixto J. Novaton
ISBN: 978-4-902837-22-3

This work is intended for all those that wish to connect to spiritual divine energies, and forces. This is for those wishing to forge a relationship with ancestor, spirit guides, angels, divinities, and deities through devout spiritual devotion. It all begins with the erection of a spiritual altar, or shrine in your home. Dedicating one hour a week to solemn devoted prayer, this will soon become ritual, the ritual turns into a connection; and enlightenment is achieved.

Once, enlightenment is achieved come the next step, which is communication by way of divination. Through divination the communication, revelations, or messages become clarified, so verification and proof of your spirituality working is achieved. These selected prayers will nourish people's psyches. provide protection, and take people's spirituality to a higher level.

How to Order blue ocean press books:

blue ocean press books can be ordered on **www.blueoceanpublications.com**, at your neighborhood bookstore, or via on of the book distributors, wholesalers, bookstores, and online bookstores listed below.

Volume Discount:
Individual Buyers: An order of 5 or more of a single title receives a 30% wholesaler discount.
Retail and Institutional Buyers: Receive a 40% discount for purchases.

Please contact us at: **wholesale@blueoceanpublications.com** to receive a discounted invoice.

blue ocean press titles can also be obtained from the following distributors:

US:
Ingram, Amazon.com, Baker & Taylor, Barnes & Noble, NACSCORP, Espresso Book Machine

UK:
Adlibris.com, Amazon.co.uk, Bertrams, Blackwell, Book Depository, Coutts, Gardners, Mallory International, Paperback Shop, Eden Interactive Ltd., Aphrohead

Additional amazon.com sites:
Brazil: amazon.com.br; Canada: amazon.ca;
China: amazon.cn; France: amazon.fr; India: amazon.in
Italy: amazon.it; Germany: amazon.de; Japan:amazon.co.jp;
Mexico: amazon.com.mx; Spain: amazon.es

We also have printers in Australia, Germany, and Brazil, so titles can be ordered within the local book distribution system in Australia, Germany, and Brazil.

www.ingramcontent.com/pod-product-compliance
Lightning Source LLC
Chambersburg PA
CBHW020346130626
46549CB00003B/1326